Be the Best at Reading

TOP TIPS

Rebecca Rissman

Raintree

Chicago, Illinois

www.capstonepub.com
Visit our website to find out more information about Heinemann-Raintree books.

To order:
☎ Phone 800-747-4992
💻 Visit www.capstonepub.com
to browse our catalog and order online.

© 2013 Heinemann Library
an imprint of Capstone Global Library, LLC
Chicago, Illinois

Visit our website at www.heinemannraintree.com

Edited by Rebecca Rissman, Dan Nunn, and Adrian Vigliano
Designed by Joanna Malivoire
Original illustrations © Capstone Global Library Ltd.
Picture research by Ruth Blair
Production by Alison Parsons
Originated by Capstone Global Library
Printed in China by CTPS

16 15 14 13 12
10 9 8 7 6 5 4 3 2 1

Library of Congress Cataloging-in-Publication Data
Rissman, Rebecca.
  Be the best at reading / Rebecca Rissman.
    p. cm.—(Top tips)
  Includes bibliographical references and index.
  ISBN 978-1-4109-4768-0 (hb)—ISBN 978-1-4109-4773-4 (pb) 1. Reading (Elementary)—Juvenile literature. I. Title.
  LB1573.R535 2013
  372.4—dc23   2011044039

Acknowledgments
The author and publishers are grateful to the following for permission to reproduce copyright material: Shutterstock pp. 4 (© Songquan Deng), 7 (© Tom C Amon), 9 (© OLJ Studio), 21 (© Valentyn Volkov), 24 (© Loskutnikov), 29 (© vovan), 29 (© Evgeny Karandaev), 29 (© Kai Wong), 30 (© Chris102), 14 (© picturepartners), 15 (© Gladskikh Tatiana), 22 (© Szasz-Fabian Ilka Erika), 23 (© SERGEY DOLGIKH), 27 (© SergiyN). Background and design features reproduced with the permission of Shutterstock.

Cover photograph reproduced with the permission of Shutterstock and Shutterstock/© notkoo.

We would like to thank Nancy Harris for her invaluable help in the preparation of this book.

Every effort has been made to contact copyright holders of any material reproduced in this book. Any omissions will be rectified in subsequent printings if notice is given to the publisher.

Disclaimer
All the Internet addresses (URLs) given in this book were valid at the time of going to press. However, due to the dynamic nature of the Internet, some addresses may have changed, or sites may have changed or ceased to exist since publication. While the author and publisher regret any inconvenience this may cause readers, no responsibility for any such changes can be accepted by either the author or the publisher.

Some words are shown in bold, **like this**. You can find out what they mean by looking in the glossary.

Contents

Get Going!

People read many different things every day. In fact, you probably read much more than you think! You read signs and directions. But sometimes reading can seem difficult. Learning a few simple tricks can make reading easier and more fun!

Top Tip

Get going! The more you read, the *better* you'll read! Try to spend some time reading every day. Read comic books, magazines, books, and more!

?

Test That Tip!

Try to read every day for 30 minutes. If this feels easy, try 45 minutes!

Fact or Fiction?

People read **nonfiction**, or **informational** text, to learn real facts. People read **fiction**, or stories about **imaginary** or made-up things, for fun. There are many different **genres**, or kinds of writing. It can be hard to remember whether a genre is nonfiction or fiction.

Top Tip

Just sound it out! Fiction starts with an F, and so does the word Fantasy. When you remember Fiction and Fantasy, then you can remember that nonfiction is *not* fantasy. Nonfiction is real.

So Many Genres

Genres are the names for different kinds of books. There are many different genres, but most fall into these four categories:

- **Informational**: Read these books to find information or facts about real things.

- **Narrative**: Read these books to find a make-believe, or **fiction**, story.

- **Opinion**: Read these books to learn the author's opinion or thoughts about something.

- **Procedural**: Read these books to learn how to do something.

Getting Started with Nonfiction Books

Nonfiction books are full of **text features** such as captions and headings. They help you find the information you want. You just need to know how to use them.

Top Tip

Table of Contents

Where is it?	Front of the book
What does it do?	Tells you what page each chapter starts on

Glossary

Where is it?	Back of the book
What does it do?	Tells you the **definition**, or meaning, of words in the book

Contents

Some words are shown in bold, **like this**. You can find out what they mean by looking in the glossary.

Glossary

agility ability to stop and change directions very quickly

balance to hold your body steady

coordination ability to get different parts of the body to work well together

cramps pains you can get when muscles tighten suddenly

hand-eye coordination ability to make your hands react to what your eyes are seeing

heat stroke when the body gets too hot and cannot cool down

immune system parts of your body that help you fight off illness

protein substance in food that gives the body energy and helps it grow. Eggs, meat, nuts, and beans have protein in them.

sprint run very fast for a short distance

stamina power to keep going or keep doing something

static still or fixed position

Look Closely on Each Page

Take a close look at the pages in a **nonfiction** book. Each page has **text features** to help you find what you are looking for.

Top Tip

Try to spot these text features:

Page numbers: These tell you where you are in the book.

Headings: These tell you what information will be on the page.

Fact boxes: These give you extra information.

Test That Tip!

Find each of the features listed on page 12!

Always wear a helmet when you ride a bike or skateboard.

9

Be Safe

Becoming more **coordinated** doesn't just happen overnight. It takes time and patience to develop skills. When you begin to learn new things, think of safety first. If you want to learn to catch a baseball, use a soft ball that won't hurt if it hits you.

Becoming better at sports is lots of fun—as long as it is done safely.

8

Scan for Information

Sometimes you read **nonfiction** books for **research**, or to learn about something specific. When you are looking for specific information, **scan**, or quickly look, for **text features**.

Top Tip

Scan the text for chapter titles, headings, and fact boxes. When you have found what you are looking for, then you can re-read for specific details.

Get the Picture!

Many **nonfiction** books use **images**, or pictures, to help you understand more about the facts. Many **fiction** books include images to help you imagine the story better. In addition to the images, books include other **text features** to give you more information.

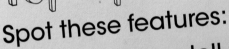

Top Tip

Spot these features:

- **Labels**: These tell you what is shown in the images.
- **Captions**: These tell you what is happening in the images.
- **Graphs and charts**: These show you numbers or amounts.

You Do the Math

You can find the height of tall trees and buildings using geometry and **ratios**. The distance from the base point to the woman is 5 meters (A). The distance from the base point to the tree is 50 meters (B). From the base point, the top of the woman's head lines up with the top of the tree. The diagram shows two **right triangles**. The ratio of the woman's height to distance A is the same as the ratio of the tree's height to distance B.

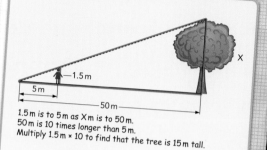

1.5 m is to 5 m as X m is to 50 m.
50 m is 10 times longer than 5 m.
Multiply 1.5 m × 10 to find that the tree is 15 m tall.

?

Test That Tip!

Find each of the features listed in the Top Tip on page 16!

What Is a Great Circle?

We're taking a trip from San Francisco, California, to London, England. The airline company wants to follow the shortest route to save jet fuel. Of course, they must consider air traffic and storms, but the fastest route around the Earth is along a **great circle**.

The shortest distance around the Earth is along a great circle.

If you look at a map of the world, you can draw a line from San Francisco to London. The route seems to be a good one, but there is a problem. The Earth is not flat like the map. It is more like a **sphere**. We should plan a route based on the shape of the Earth, not on a flat map.

10

Reading Online

You might do a lot of your reading on the **Internet**. The Internet is an online network you can find on your computer or mobile reader. Online texts have different **text features** from books or magazines.

Top Tip

Learn online text features!

- **Links**: Click on links, or buttons, to go to a new page for more information. Remember, never click on a link that you don't trust.

- **Audio**: Click on audio or sound icons to hear a person talk or listen to a recorded noise. An icon is a small picture button on a computer screen.

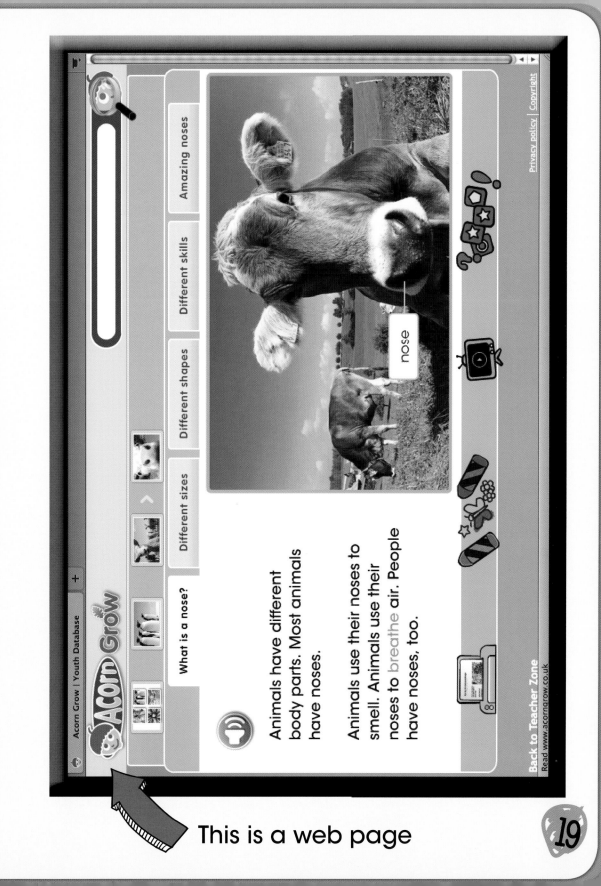

Acorn Grow | Youth Database
Acorn Grow
What is a nose?
Different sizes
Different shapes
Different skills
Amazing noses
Animals have different body parts. Most animals have noses.
Animals use their noses to smell. Animals use their noses to breathe air. People have noses, too.
nose
Back to Teacher Zone
Read www.acorngrow.co.uk
Privacy policy | Copyright

This is a web page

Searching Online

If you're looking for something specific on the **Internet**, you can use a **search engine**. Search engines can be found on pages on the Internet called web pages.

Top Tip

Follow these simple rules when you're typing words into a search engine:

- Use simple terms, like "red apple."
- Use descriptive words, like "fresh red apple."
- Don't worry about using upper-case or lower-case letters.

Is It Reliable?

The **Internet** is overflowing with information. But not all of it is **reliable**, or something you can trust. This means you need to learn to tell the difference between Internet sources that you trust and those that you should avoid.

www.

Top Tip

Web addresses are the letters and numbers found in the address bar at the top of a computer screen. Many helpful web addresses end in:

- edu
- org
- gov

Reading Directions

We read directions, or **procedural** text, every day. Directions can be found in recipes and instructions. They can be found in anything that asks you do something in a specific order.

Top Tip

Follow the numbers. Always do the steps in order.

?

Test That Tip!

Which step do you do first?
Making an apple snack:

1. Cut up an apple.
2. Spread peanut butter onto apple slices.
3. Dip apple slices into raisins.
4. Eat and enjoy!

Reading Opinions

Some books, magazine articles, or online web pages feature opinion writing. This writing often focuses on one author's opinion. You need to remember that you are only reading one person's thoughts about something.

Top Tip

When reading an author's opinion, ask yourself: "Do I agree?" If you do agree, you might want to read more. If you don't agree, it's okay. But you might want to learn more about that person's opinion and why you do not agree.

Study Like a Pro!

Set yourself up to succeed by practicing these tips when you do your homework or study.

Top Tip

Before you get to work, always:

Eat a healthy snack.

Turn off the television.

Make sure you have all the supplies you need:

- books
- dictionary
- highlighter
- pencil and note paper

Dream Big!

Remember, reading is important because we do it all the time! You might use it in your job as an actor, doctor, or pilot. The better you can become at reading, the more you will enjoy it!

What can you do to become a better reader today?

Glossary

audio something with sound. Some Websites include audio that you can play.

definition what a word means

fiction about imaginary events or people

genre category of writing, such as narrative, opinion, or procedural

image picture

imaginary not real

informational genre that teaches you about a topic

Internet computer network connecting Websites, e-mail, and databases

link button on a web page that takes you to a new page, or shows you a feature such as an audio clip

narrative genre that tells a story

nonfiction based on facts

opinion genre that communicates the writer's opinion, or personal feelings

procedural genre that shows you how to do something

reliable something you can trust

research to investigate or study something

scan read very quickly

search engine place to find information online. Search engines work best when you use specific keywords in your search

text feature elements in a text such as labels or captions that add information

Find Out More

Books

Blackaby, Susan. *Word of the Day* (Read It! Readers: Language Arts). Mankato, MN: Picture Window Books, 2009.

Somervill, Barbara A. *Studying and Tests* (School Project Survival Guides). Chicago: Heinemann Library, 2009.

Internet sites

Facthound offers a safe, fun way to find Internet sites related to this book. All of the sites on Facthound have been researched by our staff.

Here's all you do:

Visit *www.facthound.com*

Type in this code: 9781410947680

Index